Narrow

it

Down

David J. Bates

abbott press®

A DIVISION OF WRITER'S DIGEST

Narrow It Down

Abbott Press books may be ordered through booksellers or by contacting:

Abbott Press
1663 Liberty Drive
Bloomington, IN 47403
www.abbottpress.com
Phone: 1-866-697-5310

Because of the dynamic nature of the Internet, any web addresses or
links contained in this book may have changed since publication and
may no longer be valid. The views expressed in this work are solely those
of the author and do not necessarily reflect the views of the publisher,
and the publisher hereby disclaims any responsibility for them.

Any people depicted in stock imagery provided by Thinkstock are
models, and such images are being used for illustrative purposes only.

Certain stock imagery © Thinkstock.

ISBN: 978-1-4582-0693-0 (sc)
ISBN: 978-1-4582-0692-3 (e)

Library of Congress Control Number: 2012921787

ALL PHOTOS courtesy of Lisa Gunter Austin Photography.
All rights reserved. Used with permission.

Printed in the United States of America

Abbott Press rev. date: 11/16/2012

Contents

Preface

Generally speaking, education reaches into many facets of our lives. It is not finished when we are done with college. My experiences within the teaching field have yielded tremendous results in a short period of time. I wrote this book to tell of my philosophies in education, gathered through the success of my school's Leadership Cadet Corps program. Such philosophies can be applied to all aspects of life. It gives an account of how a myriad of ideas can be achieved through a "no excuses" self-commitment and a realization that we are all connected. By offering a new set of ideas for the educational system, we are giving our children the key to the American dream.

Acknowledgments

Elena Bates and Laney Bates
The Bates and Luna Families
The Barth Family
Bill and Betty Coker
Stephanie Escobar
Dolores Hoffman, Contributor
Colleen Lowry
Kyle Richardson
U.S. Congressman Pete Sessions
Major Morris Shepherd
Carlotta Thomas
The Vazquez Family
Bob Womer

Introduction

Corporal David Bates heard the door open to his office at the Thomas C. Marsh Middle School Leadership Cadet Corps building in Dallas, Texas. When he looked up, Mrs. Coker stood in the doorway. She was all of four feet nine inches tall and holding a cookie tin in one hand and a cane in the other. As a neighbor of the school, she would always bring the students and teachers homemade cookies at the start of the school year, as well as donations for their program.

"May I come in, Mr. Bates?" she asked.

"Of course, Mrs. Coker," David said, pulling up a chair for her.

"I realize I didn't call first, but I assumed you would be here," she said, hanging the cane on the edge of the chair.

"I'm always available for you. What brings you by today?"

Mrs. Coker handed him the tin of cookies.

"I wanted to drop this by. Good luck with the new school year; my husband and I love what you're doing with the kids. They always look so neat and polished." She smiled. "And here is something from us."

It was a three-hundred-dollar check.

"Thank you so much. We appreciate you and your husband. How is he?"

"Well, his cancer has come back, but he starts his treatments on Tuesday. He feels good, and that's all that matters."

"Please give my regards, and tell him anything he needs, please let me know. My students and I will see that he gets it," David said, helping her up.

As she went to leave, she inquired about the glass case with two old World War II covers behind his desk. David explained it was the start of a museum that he intended to build.

"I wish you much luck," she said.

"Thank you, Mrs. Coker; I'll have one of my students help you out."

The next morning, David and his fifty cadets made cards out of construction paper that said, "Thank you very much for the donation and the cookies. We are thinking of your husband. God Bless."

A week later, David received a telephone call from Mr. Coker, who expressed the desire to meet.

The next day, Mr. and Mrs. Coker were sitting in David's office.

"Tell me about your museum idea," Mr. Coker said.

David explained the idea of creating a museum in the Leadership Cadet Corps building to honor the veterans. It would also serve as a place for the local schools to hold free field trips and learn about the veterans as well as see the artifacts on display from the different wars.

"Well, we want to help you build it," Mr. Coker said, handing David a check for ten thousand dollars.

CHAPTER 1

In the Beginning

My teaching career started with a chance meeting the day I left active duty in 1998. It was my last day on base. I had started the morning thinking of ways to earn a living. Excited about the freedom I was about to experience, yet nervous about how I was going to start my career, I packed my bags, waved good-bye to some of my buddies, and drove off the base. I was twenty-two years old and knew very little about living on my own. I had enlisted straight out of high school while still under my parents' roof. When I was in the military, my life was not my own, so this was going to be a real test. While driving down the road on Highway 35 in Killeen, Texas, I thought about how much my life had changed. My father had passed away a few years before; I no longer had my best friend to lean on; and I knew leaving the military to become a civilian was going to take some adjustment. My first plan was to go to Florida to find a job.

As I was driving, I noticed a woman on the side of the road whose car had two flat tires, so I stopped to help. It turned out she was a principal from Dallas. While I changed a tire and drove her to the local gas station for another one, she mentioned the schools in her district were planning to implement a Leadership Cadet Corps program at the middle school level and offered me an interview. I followed her straight to Dallas.

I was hired in 1999 specifically to establish a Leadership Cadet Corps program as part of an overall plan to boost student performance. Getting students engaged in school was a big part of that effort. The school had an acceptable academic record but needed a boost. It needed something new to excite the students and get them thinking there was more to school than doing classroom work and going home. We started with nothing and then began fundraising. We were able to purchase uniforms and then gathered materials for the curriculum.

A few years later, we had all types of gear, and we began winning competitions. That was when we noticed people saying, "What's going on over there?" A typical school day started with a call to attention, followed by my telling the students to take their seats. They all sat down the same way, as they were taught. Procedures were huge: the way we passed out folders, the way I went over the calendar every single day, the way students took notes, the way we sat, the way we stood, and the way we walked. Once I reinforced that regimen, it became easier. I established these procedures because kids work better and more efficiently with a routine. The discipline they gain through this type of schedule helps to sharpen their problem-solving skills.

I don't know if you've ever had a chance to stand in front of thirty teenagers, but you quickly find out that you are not the coolest person in the room. Like many people coming from college or the military into the teaching world, I had no real understanding of the old saying, "If you give an inch, they will think they are a ruler." If you go to work and you fail to make a sale, or your team fails a pitch to get the new account, you go home—beaten, but not ruined. However, in the teaching world, if you fail the kids one day, it takes two weeks to recover because you quickly learn that their future can be impacted by those fifty minutes a day you spend with them.

CHAPTER 2

No Excuses

I teach first aid, land navigation, time management, organizational skills, and history. I also teach what is called effective army writing. I always emphasize to the students that they should get into the habit of not making excuses for tasks that should be done.

We find excuses for just about everything today, for example, when students can't get their homework done on time or we can't pay a bill by the due date. Excuses are often used as crutches. It's only natural to put things off. Let's face it; no one looks forward to taking care of unpleasant responsibilities. While motivation is needed for every desirable action, it's no wonder procrastination wins. As a teacher, I worked to embrace the concept of making no excuses and instilling this in my students.

I recently gave the kids a simple task: each one had to bring a folder in for an assignment we were doing the next day. One student came in without a folder. When I asked why he didn't have it, he immediately went into excuse mode. He said his mother didn't have time to go to Walmart. I asked if he used all his resources to try to get the folder. He couldn't answer. I took him through the process and explained to him a few possibilities for obtaining the folder. His mother could have dropped him off at the bookstore across the street from the school, where he could have purchased the folder and then walked to school, or he could have asked the science teacher down the hall if he could borrow one until his mother bought a replacement.

It wasn't long ago that I had this same attitude. The army gave me a strong work ethic, unlike anything I had ever imagined, but I went into the military with the mind-set of getting something for myself without thinking of giving in return. The men I served with were from all over the country but had one thing in common: they were young and couldn't wait until they were released for the weekend. Like most soldiers, we were consumed with partying. The barracks, however, weren't big enough for recreation, so we found a loophole in the military doctrine. Married soldiers got money for off-post housing, but because most new recruits were single and Fort Hood was crowded (three men to a two-man room), a few of us wrote a proposal that would give single soldiers money for off-post housing. Luckily, we received it. We had some of the biggest parties Fort Hood had ever seen. We were like gods to the other single soldiers on base. All of them started applying before the loophole became restricted again, which happened at lightning speed. My closest buddies in the military and I think back to those days, and we often look at our best friends and joke, "Why aren't we on *Saturday Night Live*?" Like my father always said, "You can't pick your family, but you can choose your friends."

The recruits, including myself, couldn't help but find ways to get out of doing things. One morning, there were three groups of runners placed according to speed. I was put in the fastest group. Before setting out for our run, an older first sergeant came up to the deck and informed us he was joining the fast group for the run. Our group of new recruits took off running with the sergeant. Mile three came and went, as did mile four, and by mile five, some recruits started falling out. I saw two of my friends fall out, which made it easy for me to follow suit. When I got back to the barracks, the first sergeant was waiting for the recruits to file in, thirty, forty, even fifty seconds behind. He had us stand at ease and then asked the first private why he fell out. The private responded by saying he didn't feel well after waking that morning. The sergeant told him to take his ass over to the slow group. He asked the second private why he fell out. The private responded by saying he didn't have time to eat his dinner the night before and felt weak during the run. The sergeant responded by telling him to take his ass over to the slow group too. He then asked me why I fell out, to which I responded, "I don't have an excuse, First Sergeant."

"Damn right you don't have any excuse; now get your ass with the fast group, and don't you ever fall out of a run again!" I took that as an opportunity to stay with the fast group and excel. Your parents give you so many chances to get things right. In the real world, the saying is, "Fool me once, shame on you; fool me twice, your ass is fired!" It's what we do with those chances that separate the winners from the losers.

After the first sergeant gave me a second try, my section sergeant, the platoon section leader, took a chance on me and made me a squad leader. I would lead the platoon in physical training for him in the soaking rain while he sat in his car. After I finished working the men out, he would roll down his window, maybe a centimeter, and give his instructions on what to do next. I used to say, "I hate that SOB." However, that Sergeant knew that his section was the best and we worked for him, and therefore the military benefited from it. The sergeant could tell you every word that was in every doctrine of every book. For example, he would say, "Page 11, sect B, paragraph 2" and would recite it, verbatim. His favorite ritual was to stir together Pepto-Bismol and Jack Daniels in the morning before physical training. Under his command, I learned to respect my elders and more important, I learned what the phrase "Do as I say and not as I do" really means. He showed us the path to becoming men and women of honor and integrity.

While the other section sergeant would take older, more experienced soldiers for his division, my Sergeant picked new recruits and gave them the responsibilities that only the older soldiers were entitled to. Making us young recruits step up in a hurry and with a sense of urgency trained us to outperform everyone else and rise to the challenge.

If you tell soldiers they have to take that hill, the mind-set is they have to accomplish this mission, no excuses.

Of course, in the earlier example of the student without the folder, the particular task is not as important as the chance to teach this student that most things can be accomplished if determination is behind the action. It may be just enough of a lesson for him to realize that it's possible to get better grades or to make college happen, even though his parents cannot afford it or support is not given at home. The earlier students prepare for the challenges of college entry, the better. That means teaching them to think and problem-solve on their own.

The College Board Advocacy Center did a comprehensive study based on research with 1,000 parents and 1,250 students of low- and moderate-income backgrounds. It underscores families' urgent need for earlier information about the cost of college and the resources available to help them afford it. Fewer than half the parents were confident that they knew the cost to attend a public college in their home state. They had even less awareness of Pell Grant programs. Resources and outside help become options for those students who go through the thought process of "no excuses." Practice itself does not make perfect, but perfect practice makes perfect.

Although the military taught me the "no excuses" rule, Kyle Richardson drove home that point for me when I first started to teach. Kyle Richardson is a high school principal. Before that, he worked his way up from elementary principal to middle school principal. He surrounds himself with good and loyal people committed to making the educational system push students harder and help them realize their potential. It's one thing to manage kids; it's another to manage adults. Good teachers can discipline their class through a facial expression, but adults need to hear the words and, in the absence of good leadership, they will follow anyone. There's an old illustration of a wagon, and sitting on top are some of the oldest but wisest people who no longer are able to pull. There are the ones out front, sweating and bleeding but pulling their weight. Then there are the ones who claim to do it better than anyone, all the while sitting on the back of the wagon, dragging their feet. Kyle is the man who sees the importance of the past and the need for the future. He will hit the biggest bump in the road to knock off the dead weight. He builds good relationships for a common goal and allows teachers to dream big. When asked about an idea for the Leadership Cadet Corps building, he said, "Let's build it." I proceeded to list the obstacles, to which, he replied, "Those barriers shouldn't stop you from building." There is no doubt that one day, Principal Richardson will build up his high school to be one of the best in the nation.

CHAPTER 3

Above and Beyond

It is easy for teachers to go above and beyond in their teaching careers. Every teacher knows someone who works year round. Teachers have a 185-day contract. They have one week off for Thanksgiving, two weeks off for Christmas, three-day weekends for Labor Day, Memorial Day, Presidents' Day, and Martin Luther King Jr. Day, and let us not forget spring break and the entire summer off. As a teacher, I understand we put in many hours outside the classroom—parent-teacher conferences and after-school activities, just to name a couple of activities. It can be exhausting after a full day with children, but add up all the extra hours and it still does not compare to working all year round like most Americans. Teachers can go beyond with ease. Going above and beyond from a teacher's standpoint means investing extra effort into what he or she can control, such as staying after school to tutor, or brainstorming with an administrator on a new program.

Every teacher is allowed a planning and collaborative meeting period. It's a chance for the teachers to share information about similar students. The results speak for themselves. According to the Association for Supervision and Curriculum Development (ASCD), schools that connect teacher learning to student learning often have a better chance of making a positive impact on student achievement. Collaborative planning provides opportunities for teachers to work together to make those connections through examining their practice, consulting with colleagues, and developing their skills. Collaborative planning requires making the time to work and learn with colleagues. Many schools are finding ways to incorporate teacher collaboration into the school day. Some suggestions follow:

- Develop a master schedule to allow students to have longer instructional periods with fewer teachers and teachers to have shared planning time.
- For schools that have year-round calendars, use gaps between sessions for multiple-day meetings focused on teacher planning.
- Ensure that faculty; team, department, and grade-level meetings are opportunities for collaborative planning and learning rather than meetings focused on administration and management details.

Of course, district administrators and teachers should work together in developing collaboration opportunities and ensuring that teacher collaboration time is valued time, focused on improving teaching and learning.

One reality of the teaching profession is that there is no such thing as a corner office. In the business world, you start at the bottom and work your way up to manager and then director and so on. Some very famous people have done just that.

Have you ever wondered who Famous Amos is? While living with his aunt and going to school, Wally Amos loved the homemade cookies she always made. He got a job at the William Morris Agency working in the mailroom at first and then became the first African-American agent. He would send cookies to his clients and invite them to visit. After getting a loan for twenty-five thousand dollars and creating his own chocolate-chip cookie recipe, he launched the first Famous Amos store in 1975.

Every position in life and business holds responsibility and accountability; in most areas, a person must work his or her way up the scale. This is not so true in education though. Working your way up the different levels of teaching before you are entrusted with the education of an entire campus should be the goal in school districts. If this were the military and an eighteen-year-old private could take a test and go from squad member to company commander in less than three years, we might win two out of ten battles. Offering more responsibility and more liability will only make people work harder to obtain those types of higher positions. For an example of this idea, let's examine two English teachers. One excels at his or her job and receives excellent results from the students. The other one skates by and consistently receives below-average grades from his or her students, mostly because of failure to communicate the curriculum effectively. Both receive the same salary and are evaluated the same. How long do you think it will take before the excellent teacher throws up his or her hands and says, "Why should I work so hard?" In this example, there is no motivation and no morale boosting to keep this teacher on the path to success. This would never last in the business world for very long; why should it be allowed or tolerated in schools?

CHAPTER 4

ROTC Defined

ROTC stands for Reserve Officer Training Corps. This is a college program. JROTC (Junior ROTC) is the high school program, and the middle school program is called LCC (Leadership Cadet Corps). According to Title 10, Section 2031 of the US Code, the purpose of JROTC is to instill in students the values of citizenship, service to the United States, and personal responsibility and a sense of accomplishment. The objectives are:

- Developing good citizenship and patriotism
- Developing self-reliance, leadership, and responsiveness to constituted authority
- Improving the ability to communicate well both orally and in writing
- Developing an appreciation of the importance of physical fitness
- Increasing a respect for the role of US Armed Forces in support of national objectives
- Developing knowledge of team-building skills and basic military skills
- Taking three to four years of the course allows the

cadets to instantly rank higher if they pursue a military career.

I hope I didn't lose you, but I wanted to state the official definition of ROTC. It also states that JROTC should provide meaningful leadership instruction of benefit to the student and of value to the Armed Forces. The JROTC and NDCC (National Defense Cadet Corp) are not, in and of themselves, officer-producing programs but should create favorable attitudes and impressions toward the Services and toward careers in the Armed Forces.

In his 1995 autobiography "My American Journey" General Colin Powell said, "The armed forces might get a youngster more inclined to enlist as a result of Junior ROTC," and added that "inner-city kids, many from broken homes, found stability and role models in Junior ROTC."

The first JROTC brigade in the nation was started at Leavenworth High School in Kansas in 1916.

CHAPTER 5

The Patriot

Here's an idea: why not implement patriot classes as part of the curriculum at the elementary, secondary, or even the college level. It would be extremely beneficial to help expand our knowledge of this country as a whole. Most people, if asked, would not be able to tell you the history of the flag, what the stars or stripes stand for, even the meaning of the "Star-Spangled Banner." They may not even know how to salute the flag. It is easy to teach children about their heritage, but we forget the fact that we should teach them about the United States. As citizens, we should know the record of our country, the good and the bad. If you plan to move to a new neighborhood, you research the area first. You research the ratings of the schools, the crime rate, and the location of the nearest grocery stores so you have an idea of where you will be living. That is no different than knowing the history of your country. Having said that, the decision to have a separate class or incorporate it with American history is up to the individual school district. Either way, it is an opening for dialogue and creates a sense of patriotic camaraderie. The benefits extend from the students to the country.

On April 10, 2003, Pulitzer Prize winner David McCullough told a Senate committee, "We are raising a generation of people who are historically illiterate ... We can't function in a society," he continued, "If we don't know who we are and where we came from." This profound yet simple statement should serve as a wake-up call to us, as a country. Remembering that the American flag is an idea and a symbol, rather than just a cloth representation of our country, lends credibility to the importance of making patriot classes an option at any age.

CHAPTER 6

Where Are the Men?

It seems that society has been lacking more than just a few good men lately. For the past twenty years, common courtesies that were given regularly have been going extinct—the holding of the door; refraining from cursing in the presence of women, older people, and children; and men asking women on a date, to name a few. I am fully aware that women can do anything on their own. However, when I see a woman carrying a box from her car to the school, I offer to help. Sometimes, the answer is "I got it, thanks," and sometimes, they appreciate the offer. The point is, you should at least offer. Because of my military days, I clean the house, sweep, and vacuum, whatever it takes to get the job done. I like the feeling of providing and helping someone. My wife and I work together to provide for our family. If my daughter needs fifty dollars for soccer, I can provide and it gives me pride. But the male gender has been emasculated over the years. I'm not sure if it's the culture they grew up in or if it's that no one was there to teach them about becoming a man. Too many children come from divorced families and have a single parent raising them. It is incredibly hard, if not impossible. Hats off to the women who work so hard to try, but role modeling is the key to success here. Men are more distant from a family or their children than they have ever been. The out-of-wedlock birthrate is over 40 percent in America. In 1960, only 11 percent of children in the United States lived apart from their fathers, in 2010 that figure grew to 27 percent.

My friend was raised by a strong mother who told him that women are intelligent and independent and didn't need any special treatment. I agree with most of this—except the part about special treatment. I believe that all women should be treated as special. They are the mothers of our children, the caretakers of the sick in the house (especially mine, since I become a baby when I get sick), and jacks-of-all-trades. My friend always tells me that when he goes on a date, he respects the woman but doesn't offer to hold the door open or pay for dinner. He splits the check with her because he wants her to feel strong and independent. As you can imagine, he doesn't get second dates. Why? Because regardless of gender, common courtesy is nice, offering is nice, and everyone likes to feel special. The same holds true with older people. If I see my eighty-year-old neighbor struggling to walk down his driveway to get the paper, I'll get it for him. Opening the door for someone, whether male or female, is the right thing to do. Men are afraid to overstep their bounds for fear they will be viewed as sexist. Do it anyway. Open doors, pay for dinners, and if you can help older people in need, help them. Pick up that paper in the driveway, and help the woman juggling five bags. If they hit you over the head for doing it, move on and keep doing it.

Most young men today don't even know some common considerations, such as removing their hat in church or during the national anthem. This may seem dated, but it's a simple act of civility that shows respect. The other day, I walked into a meeting where three men were sitting. As I went to shake their hands, two of them remained seated. Show some respect and stand up to shake someone's hand. That was such a big deal to me that I was thinking to myself, "Who does this guy think he is, the godfather?" In this day and age, all I'm asking is for the real men to stands up.

CHAPTER 7

The Corps

As for us at Thomas C. Marsh Middle School, we build citizenship, time management, military history, courtesy and customs, drill and ceremony and organizational skills. The cadets will perform an exhibition where they carry out elaborate maneuvers. Armed drill team entails an inspection of their weapons, marching together, and spinning and flipping the rifles. We also have a color guard team that consists of two rifles and two flags, the American flag and the state flag. They march together as a unit and submit colors. At the end, we have what is called a knockout, where every cadet is given commands until there is only one left standing. In addition, the top five girls and boys compete against others from different schools in physical training. Rank structure is the same as in the military in that you are ranked based on nothing but hard work and knowledge. You work your way up from private to private first class to specialist and then to corporal. Inside of these ranks are leadership positions of responsibility. The cadets have to go in front of the board, and the graduating class has to pick the next commanding officer. This competitive environment builds confidence and character.

A perfect example of this is Major Shepherd. There is Superman; there is Batman; and then there is Major Shepherd, a retired African-

American soldier, who spent twenty years in the military, where he would frequently pull twenty-four-hour shifts. He is also a true family man. I met Major Shepherd when he was the Deputy Director of Army Instruction. As the DDAI, he handles high school JROTC programs. He saw a need for a stronger Leadership Cadet Corps program at our middle school campuses and made it happen. He sought help from people around him and below his rank, like me, a corporal. He is not afraid to ask, "What can we do to better this program?" He is the real deal and made it clear that it is all about the cadets. We were all teaming up to introduce a curriculum handbook and create more effective teaching strategies and more opportunities for instructors to showcase their programs. In his first summer working with the middle schools, he started taking ownership of the program and participation grew. He saw to it that the instructors were committed to making sure students went from middle school LCC to high school JROTC.

Major Shepherd is the type of person to go into a conference and speak in the same uniform he wore in the seventies alongside a man in a suit and tie. There is something to be said for a person who is genuine. What comes out of his mouth is straight from his head, without a filter. Sometimes, that's good, and sometimes, that's bad, but he doesn't sugarcoat issues. No one leaves the room unsure about his thoughts. He's a man who can handle ten thousand tasks in a day, yet cannot remember where he set his phone down or where he left his car keys. That makes him human. A father figure, Major Shepherd taught me to surround myself with people who can better the life around me—a lesson I now teach to my students. He always encourages instructors to focus in on what works, which leads me to my thoughts on marquee programs. A marquee program is similar to a football franchise. If you have a program in your school that you think could be the next great thing for the kids or your community, you should find a person who shares that vision and let him or her run with it. Thirteen years ago, our middle school had low test scores, our ratings were tanking, and we had low-income and high-crime neighborhoods in our district. We started the Leadership Cadet Corps. program with seventy-eight students. The kids loved it, and we focused our attention on expansion. We are now up to four hundred students, or one-third of our school's population. With our cadets taking pride and sharing the power with others, the gang presence disappeared because there were more kids in the Leadership Cadet Corps program than in the gangs. Since they were part of a program, they started to think differently. They passed tests and achieved goals because the advantages of passing were more than just doing well. In taking those grades home and feeling proud to share them with their families, they continued to excel. Many schools use sports as their program, which is a great idea, as are band and academic programs.

The LCC program was in full swing, and there was another teacher in the building who was also the band leader. He was very good at motivating students. He took a hundred students and added two hundred more within three years. All of a sudden, our marquee programs spilled over to other programs, and they are driving the academic aspect too because students are not just involved with going to school and going home, they have invested interest. When a person is invested, he or she will bend over backward to succeed. My commanding officer, whose father is in jail and whose mother has five children to raise on a low income, is now a volleyball player, cheerleader, and an LCC commander. If there weren't a marquee program for her to be a part of, she probably wouldn't do any of it; she'd just be another girl walking the halls, coming to school and going home. But now she goes to school from seven to seven, and guess what; she is proud, and it spills over to her little brothers and sisters, so the whole "my father's in jail" excuse is not preventing her from doing whatever she wants with her life.

Another student, who became the first female commanding officer of the LCC program, took that role seriously. With Stephanie's first year in the program, she focused in on building our LCC facility, since that was our main concern. We came in second at nationals the following year. That didn't sit well with Stephanie. The next year, when the local news channel interviewed us, she promised we would get our title back. After we raised enough money to go to Kansas to compete for the national title, Stephanie's determination resulted in a comeback, and the team reclaimed the title. She is now at the high school trying to graduate in the top 10 percent of her class of over four hundred students. Her experience was expressed in a letter she wrote in September 2011, which is presented in the next chapter.

CHAPTER 8

Stephanie's Testimony

Life can be so great and rewarding at times. The things you learn every day can be the most precious lessons. I can tell you that I now look back at my life starting now and say, "I am strong, and I will succeed in anything I am determined to do." This mentality is one of the most important things to me because LCC has taught me this in an amazing way. There is nothing like learning from the best program in the world. I figured this out my first day of seventh-grade year.

I remember walking in the LCC portable scared. My mind was rushing with thoughts on what to do and how to speak. I just remember trying to keep my eyes on the instructor, Corporal David Bates, as I tried to soak it all in. He began to explain the program in a committed voice. I knew this was going to be something I wanted to do. I stayed focused and within a few days' practice, the biggest goal was on.

Cpl. Bates decided to put me in the advanced LCC period. I was overwhelmed with excitement. He wanted me to command their Unarmed Regulation Drill. I put my heart on the ground and ended up winning second place in my section during nationals. I was not done yet. I knew I could do better.

The next year came around, and that's when the opportunities hit. I was announced "The First Female Commanding Officer" at Marsh Middle School. My duty was to make sure that we won nationals. I did not mind at all because again, I was determined. I yelled every day and practiced like there was no tomorrow. That late March day came extremely quick. It was the second nationals I was attending, better said, commanding. This time, it was in Kansas. I knew that we were not going to let this go to waste. We performed with our hearts and drilled with our soul. No matter what we did, we did not give up during the unfair disqualifications.

At the decisive moment, I was shocked. We were titled National Champions 2010. I knew we gave our best, yet I was amazed. All this amounted to making me realize what it meant to be committed. This life lesson let us know that we can achieve anything we decide if we set our minds to it. I set my mind in making sure we won nationals. I can say my everything was in it. I was only thirteen years old. That is still bizarre to me because people do not realize how your dreams can come true with sweat and hard work. When I put my uniform on, it's an amazing feeling. I am proud of myself and it makes you feel like you're actually doing something for your community. I think that's important.

It's the most exciting thing. You're out there, everyone sees you, and they don't just see you as this person. They see you as a cadet at Marsh Middle School.

—Stephanie Escobar

Stephanie Escobar is the perfect example of attaining the

American dream. Tony Vazquez is another one. Tony's family came from Mexico, worked hard, and stayed on top of their children to do well. Tony was a cadet in the Leadership Cadet Corps program and went on to college. His classes are at night because during the day, he gives back. He helps me with the students and receives little pay. He wants to be the first Hispanic governor of the State of Texas someday, and I believe he will succeed. He is the proven product of what can be done in this country.

Because of our first marquee program, our school's other programs are growing: band is good; choir is good; and now drama is starting. It has gone from twenty-six students to ninety-seven and counting. Marquee programs don't have to be on a national championship level, but they have to be where someone in charge can motivate the students to do well. Once that happens, it will spill over to other aspects of life.

Currently, ROTC classes are offered to every student in this country with an array of financial benefits toward college tuition. This program can easily work with many financial aid plans already in existence. Earning, not giving, is the point, which leads me to talk about entitlement.

CHAPTER 9

Sense of Entitlement

A sense of entitlement is rampant. It seems we've gone from promoting self-esteem, beginning in the early seventies, to morphing that into entitlement in the modern day. The notion of us feeling entitled is fueled largely by what we see on television and in the classrooms. Most children have cell phones by the age of ten. They also have televisions in their rooms, along with iPods and Xboxes. The latest gadgets are always around the corner and feeding the never-ending appetite for technology of adults and children. It is not to say that having a desire for such things is bad, but there is something to be said for waiting for it until you have earned it. When we give something to our children or accept something without working for it, over time, we start to settle into a privileged state of mind. It's kind of like the person who stands on a bluff in Hawaii overlooking a pristine beach and complains that his last vacation was better. I want my students and my daughter to realize that entitlement only exists for someone who earns it. When a student is given the proper education but consistently fails to hand in his or her homework, a teacher should not give him or her one more day to finish it or take ten points off.

The sense of entitlement within the student body has escalated within the last five years. It is intolerable and destructive to a student's education to let him or her slide. Unfortunately, it has been going on for years, and we are seeing the effects with our young adults today. When you send your children to school, they are supposed to get the proper education. What is not supposed to happen is the teacher giving it away instead of making the kids earn it. I am not saying that unless you sit up straight in class, I will not teach this assignment or that giving them a break could change the outcome of how they perform in your class, but when the students have the material to do their schoolwork and fail to turn it in and then you give them two weeks more or reduce the grade, you're not teaching them accountability. Entitlement is becoming somewhat of an epidemic. We need to give them the best education, but they in return have to earn it. Respect and giving by accomplishing should be every school's mission. I may see the scrappiest project cross my desk, but as long as the student produced it on his or her own and used all his or her resources, that student deserves a high grade.

In my LCC class, rich or poor, students earn their uniforms the same way, along with their rank. A rich kid in the military gets treated the same as a poor kid. Everyone is green; no one is color. Everyone has a last name and rank on the front of his or her uniform, and all have the opportunity to move up the same way. The entitlement mentality will cripple our thinking when applying for a job and hiring other people.

By implementing this, you will hear less of the "poor me" syndrome. For example, if I have to get a Monopoly game to teach math, that is what I should do instead of saying, "Well, the school district didn't buy me a Monopoly game." You are not always entitled by virtue of being a teacher either. It will come back; test scores will improve, and when that happens, you look good. If you look good, the principal looks good, and if the principal looks good, the district looks good, and you will stay employed. I believe we all feel the same way. We want our kids to have better than we had growing up, but at the same time, we all make the mistake of giving our kids ice cream before dinner—which we all know is hard to fix, before they go to bed.

CHAPTER 10

Motivation Starts Early

My motivation started early in life. I was born in Point Pleasant, New Jersey, in 1976 to a family with three brothers and four sisters. I am number eight, the "baby" of the family.

My first job was laboring on a parsley farm in southern New Jersey when I was ten years old. I would cut the parsley all day and then place the bushels in bags of ice. Young and tired, I did that for an entire week and received fifty dollars and a minor case of parsley poison to my hands. I considered it a lot of money, but my father thought I deserved a lot more. I also made baseball card stands out of wood. My father and I would cut a small groove for the cards to stand upright, rent a table at the local flea market, and sell them for five dollars apiece. For me, working and earning money started early.

My family moved to Florida where I began the eighth grade as that "weird kid from the North." The fact that I played sports gave me the advantage of being able to make friends fast. I earned MVP my first year of school playing basketball and quickly became good at football and baseball. Never having much, yet never really knowing it, I was always resourceful. I drew knowledge from everyone I met. I was not that person who had hundreds of friends in high school.

I had one best friend, two close friends, and hundreds I just knew. My best friend and I had experienced freedom at a young age. Since my parents were older and a single father raised my best friend, we had liberty most kids could only dream of.

While in high school, I picked oranges in the groves for a hundred dollars a day. The huge tubs had to be filled, which was no small task. I wore a bag around my waist as I climbed the orange trees, sometimes working in tandem with my friends on the ground. Throwing the oranges down at a fast pace hurried the process. I count my Pizza Hut job as the most ridiculous. The owner, who was single and ready to mingle, was never there, so you can imagine what a crew of teenagers in a Pizza Hut with a liquor license could get themselves into. She allowed us to lock the place up at night. We had no supervision, unlimited resources to make pizzas, and kegs of beer on tap; needless to say, everyone signed up for the night shift.

While in high school, my friends and I tried our hand at gator hunting on the weekends; after all, it was Florida. We had a small boat, a few nets, and no clue what we were doing. We would jump from bridges with thirty-foot drops, not knowing what was below. My best friend's dad had a boat that we used unaccompanied. He would drive the boat to the lake, and we would water-ski and kneeboard all summer, hanging off the side occasionally. One time, we ran out of gas and had to take turns swimming and paddling the boat back to shore. We were in the water almost every day that summer.

We played all the sports in high school through the week and, without much planning, went on a trip to some part of Florida on the weekends, never getting into much trouble. In our senior year, we ended up receiving MVP honors in athletics but lagged behind in academics. Sometimes, we would arrive to school late and leave early, never having anyone say anything to us. On graduation day, we had no idea what to do next. No one prepared us for anything outside of attending school. We both received many letters from colleges, but neither of us understood how the process worked. At the same time, my father was declining in health, having battled diabetes for thirty years. He lost one of his legs and wanted to move back to New Jersey to be close to family. I joined the army while my best friend opted for the navy.

I served three years and seventeen weeks, some of that time in Georgia, California, Texas, and the Middle East. The important part about the military was that it made me a man. Regrettably, my father died before he got to know me as a man and vice versa.

Although my motivation and drive to succeed and change the world around me started early, some people find it difficult to become motivated. For me, something as easy as waking up early gets me motivated. My tasks are manageable, and my productivity is the highest at this time. There is an old saying that goes "Eat the frog first," meaning do the least favorite or most tedious task early in the day. For some, it means getting their exercise out of the way or focusing on difficult tasks. Oftentimes, the way I motivate my students is through competition. An example of this is a friendly wager with another teacher. Say both of us have exams for the students to complete. Now, I could probably walk in and tell the children that I'd talked to the math teacher down the hall and I'd bet him or her a pizza party that my students would do better on the test, and those children would jump all over it. Some critics might say competition shouldn't be a motivator. I say it should, and it works. The two classrooms will have higher scores overall. Not every child is self-motivated; sometimes, we have to come up with little strategies to help them along. When they do well on the test, the self-esteem follows. They did it for the pizza but found out that they could do fractions and ratios very easily too.

Motivation in the classroom is not always easy to figure out. What motivates one student may not necessarily work for another. In my classroom, I don't have the students competing against each other; rather, I have them working as a team. This does two things. It motivates them to achieve their goal and boosts their self-esteem, as they feel like part of a team. Whether they win or lose, they did it as a team.

When they are in middle school and high school, I believe students should have more control over what tasks they'll accomplish, as long as the job of teaching them is complete. If you give students the choice of completing a certain task on a certain day, they feel empowered, which in turn will motivate them to get the task done in a timely manner. This is not to say that all control is given to the student. But, the teacher benefits from the self-discipline of the students yet still has control. For those students who are not easily motivated, rewards can be valuable. Just as is illustrated above with the pizza party and the test example, students will respond to rewards if all else fails. In one school I visited, they gave incentives by way of contests. The students who received the highest grades were able to enjoy a trip to the ice-cream stand after lunch with the principal. The students who didn't pass received encouragement and were given another opportunity the following month.

Chapter 11

The Forefront

In 2011, our school, along with others, was featured on PBS. The segment was titled "Ending America's Dropout Crisis: Middle School Intervention That Works."

"Every year, 1.2 million American high school students do not graduate on schedule, and more than one in four fail to earn a diploma. In today's global economy, it is imperative that America improves the rate of high school graduation so that students emerge career and college ready.

They're called "drop out factories"—American high schools where fewer than 60% of students make it to graduation day. Today, about one out of every ten high schools fits the description. They are clustered in large cities and poor rural areas alike and for the more than two million students attending these drop out factories, the outlook is grim." (Glassman, 2012)

Currently, the nation has a graduation rate of right about 75 percent, which means that about a million kids a year are not getting their diplomas on time. There were four million in the class of 2010. Three million got diplomas in June. If you're in your twenties, don't have a high school degree, and don't have a work history, are you ever going to work? Probably not, but every year, we're putting a million kids toward that future.

For minority students, the problem is even more acute, with a national graduation rate of only 50 percent for African American and Hispanic students.

Dr. Lindan Hill, the dean of the Marian University School of Education, also gave an overview of the dropout crisis saying, "Just because a kid is poor, or their parents are poor, doesn't mean that they don't have a lot of ability, that they don't have a lot of potential, because they do. Poverty, economic-inequality, other kinds of inequalities mitigate against those kids having opportunities. It's not the ability that they lack. It's the opportunity." (Hill D. L., 2012)

Research shows that making sure students get those opportunities during middle school is critical to increasing graduation rates. By high school, it is difficult to turn most failing or struggling students around.

Our Marsh Middle School in Dallas, Texas, is boosting academic achievement by using student engagement both inside and outside of the classroom, and the LCC Drill Team is one of the school's hallmark programs designed to instill discipline and high expectations in students from the surrounding disadvantaged and largely minority community. My associate principal, Carlotta Thomas, stated it perfectly: "We give all students that enter into this building a chance regardless of their background, their income level, or their ethnicity. They have the opportunity to be the very best, and we insure our teachers with the skills and materials to do so. One of the reasons why we're one of the best schools in Dallas is due to our test scores, from last year. In writing we were 92 percent passing, reading we were 90 percent, math 90 percent, science 81 percent. Kids who are involved tend to have better grades and go on to graduate from college. Therefore, we do encourage them to do something besides just coming to school. We expect students to have A's or B's on report cards and we expect them to go to tutoring if they need help. We expect them to do science fair projects and to be dressed appropriately for school and to have great behavior. So anything that we want them to do, we expect them to do their very best.

This academic success didn't happen overnight.

When I came to the middle school in 1999, it wasn't the best place to work. There was a lot of gang activity as well as a lot of bullying and fighting. Our scores were low. We were everything you would think of a big, large urban school district with public-school kids.

When the kids perform for me, they perform at a high level. They don't want to let me down, so when I just put little things on the table like, "We need to do better; your scores need to be better. You better do this, or you better do that," they don't want to let me down. It's been okay not to pay their bills. It's been okay not to get a referral. It's been okay at home. That's what it's been; it's just been okay. Well, that average, okay stuff is not good enough here. I set high expectations, expectations that mirror those of the school at large.

The discipline is not what many people think discipline is. It's self-discipline, the discipline to do what is right when no one is looking. Integrity starts to come into play with some of these kids; they know they must do well, or they'll hear it.

All the teachers at Marsh Middle use job assignments to teach students responsibility and to get them invested in their own education. The kids all have jobs. When you give a kid a job, he or she takes it seriously. At our school, just passing out folders is not really a great job, but it's their job, and they take it seriously.

When students are engaged and well behaved, it is easier for teachers to do their jobs.

It's been thirteen years since I started the Leadership Cadet Corps program at Marsh Middle. I have gone from 78 to 387 students—about a third of the student body now participates in the program, and while my drill team has won numerous national championships, I am most proud of my students' high school graduation rate of 97 percent. I am not done yet though. I'm at the point now where I want to take it another step. The high school diploma is not as good as it used to be. My hopes, goals, and dreams for the students are to see 100 percent graduate from college.

We understand you're going to go to high school. Therefore, we just decided to take it a step further—to make sure that you're going to be a college graduate. I like to think my students are the best in the world, and that's 100 percent of the time—they are the best in the world when they're with me. Sometimes, when they're not with me, they're not the best in the world, but that's what we work on every day.

CHAPTER 12

Narrow It Down

There are two viewpoints on affecting the world around us that I use to draw focus on what is important. One is the "Ring of Influence" and the other is the "Ring of Concern." One directly influences people around you, and the other consumes you with few results.

Simply defined, our Ring of Concern usually focuses on such things as how much our neighbors are making, what the latest movie stars are up to, or what people are wearing. I believe these concerns take away from what we really should focus on and may be a diversion for us to take leave of our important issues for a while. We all are guilty of that. How many times have you spent a half hour on the phone or an hour with a group of friends talking about people or issues that don't concern you? You can give your opinion, but opinions don't do much. Actions do much. Now, when I say opinions, I don't mean *advice* because advice could actually help and influence people. What I'm talking about is using your time wisely. Using your Ring of Influence effectively is more important and more attainable than you may think. By simply reaching for the higher shelf at a grocery store on behalf of an older person or depositing clothes in the local Salvation Army box, you are influencing and affecting people around you for the better. You are capable of more than you think. Test yourself. Our Ring of Influence is what directly affects us, our community, and our life in general.

I admit to losing focus myself. Sometimes, it's because I need to escape all the rigors of everyday life or I think that somehow, I will be able to change and influence issues on a global scale; after all, I am a teacher. (Insert big head here.) As a teacher, my Ring of Influence involves my students, and I must consider how I can encourage them in a positive way. When those in the federal government are asked how education can be fixed, I wonder if they realize that it is way outside their Ring of Influence. Believe it or not, rehabilitation in education can only be accomplished at a local level. Most elected officials who pass the laws on education haven't seen the inside of a school in years, yet we expect them to give us an answer on how to fix education in this country. Let's start working within our own Ring of Influence.

The summer after my military career ended, I took a job at my local church. A wonderful man named Bob Womer instilled in me the importance and meaning of religion. He paid a group of us to go on a mission trip, building houses in Honduras. I felt very positive about what we accomplished in such a short period of time, but when I arrived back in Dallas, I felt slightly let down because the results were no longer in my sight. I went on another mission trip, this time to Mexico. It was then that I realized I didn't have to leave my country to build a house or dig wells for people in need. The following summer, we missioned in New York City. We duplicated the success from those missions abroad and used them locally. We started raising funds and gathering donations for clothing drives, toy drives at Christmas, and supplies for food pantries. I am not dismissing the causes and hard work done in struggling countries. I know Habit for Humanity and mission trips started by countless churches around the country play important roles in improving the quality of life for many people in these countries. For me though, my neighborhood was important enough to invest my time and energy in because no matter how often I travel, my neighborhood is my home and my future. Seeing results and improvement encourages me to continue to invest in my corner of the world. It could start small, from an idea created at a local church, the YMCA, or a women's group. Wherever it originates, the goal of improving your life starts in your own backyard. Some ways you can make a difference include coaching at your local school, donating blood, running for office within your local government, or starting groups that help residents with grief, finances, or whatever will directly change our world for the better.

By taking this concept of shifting what directly concerns him or her and applying it to the school system, a teacher can affect the kids who come into the classroom just like a therapist can affect the outcome of marriage after counseling or a coach can affect players' performances during a game. As a teacher, I am not concerned with what happened to the kids before they entered my classroom, and I don't care who had them before. If you are my student, I have the opportunity to shape your life. Look higher than that, to the principal; he or she is focused on making sure teachers have what they need to make this happen by helping the school district come up with the money for such items as laptops, projectors, and teaching materials.

Ken Barth, a friend of mine, is a self-made man. I taught his son in LCC and coached him in both football and baseball for four years. He and his wife were always at the games and helped wherever there was a need. He changed our entire athletic facility and was instrumental in finding funds to have the locker rooms painted, the old fifties carpet replaced, and the concrete stained. The list goes on and on. We even built a weight room because he found the money to get it done. He simply took care of things. His daughter became a cadet in the LCC program as well. He is a straightforward man with a good moral compass and is generous with his time and money. Once, he gave thousands of dollars to make all the LCC programs in the district successful. The funds provided uniforms to all the students, which gave them a polished look and the confidence to compete in drills. He even purchased the van we use to travel to all our competitions.

A few years ago, we decided to hold a dinner for instructors and principals to meet and talk; because of budget cuts, it was possible that some instructors were going to lose their jobs. After he hosted that dinner and highlighted the importance of these instructors, not one lost his or her job. He paid for the dinner because he knew it was necessary to get them together for the purpose of saving their employment. He and his wife also bought a three-hundred-acre organic farm outside Dallas and gave us fifty acres to use for the LCC program to include a four-room trailer, because he believes in the program and believes we are doing the right thing for the public school system. He works with a technician at his software company on school district policies, which could improve their efficiency rate in the future. All of this, he does out of his own pocket. In addition to inspiring me with his generosity, he and his wife have taught me what can be accomplished when passion is behind an action; it creates results. In contrast, there is a reporter I knew who wrote an article about a 5K run that a business was sponsoring in town. He started focusing on things outside his circle of influence. Does the business have enough water bottles to hand out? Will the runners know where to sign up? Did the business coordinate with the police department on the route the runners will take? His job was to write about the event, focusing on the charity and the winners and giving a general overview.

Sometimes, we find ourselves going toward that Ring of Concern just in case, when we are inside that Ring of Influence, things go wrong or not as planned. Oftentimes, we use it as a crutch to quit when things get tough. This focus on the Ring of Concern is nothing more than an excuse for not making something positive happen. If everybody worked to make a difference inside his or her spectrum, it would eventually get larger and larger and larger, making an impact on a global level. It starts local. It starts within your house and your community.

One other aspect of the Ring of Concern would be to prioritize what you can directly influence. This came to me in April 2008. When I was coaching girls' varsity softball, my team was undefeated and planning to attend a state playoff game one hundred miles away. I reserved a charter bus for us. When we were halfway to the game, I received a phone call. Something was wrong with my pregnant wife, and she was going to have the baby three weeks early. I quickly had the bus driver pull over to the side, where I changed my dress shoes to tennis shoes and told the girls that I was proud of them and everything that they had learned throughout the year would carry over, but on that day I couldn't physically be there with them. I grabbed my bag and waved good-bye as I hitchhiked fifty miles back to Dallas. The team and I both realized the importance of family and that my priorities had changed inside of what I could control. While at the hospital, I received a phone call. The girls were in the seventh inning, hoping for a storybook ending of winning against adversity; they were losing 13 to 0. Not one was sad or mad; instead, they were thankful for their season and my new family. Ask yourself, "What can I change?"

Bob Womer also told me a story that I often reflect on called "The Long-Handled Spoons."

The Long-Handled Spoons

A man spoke with the Lord about heaven and hell. The Lord said to the man, "Come, I will show you hell."

They entered a room where a group of people sat around a huge pot of stew. Everyone was famished, desperate, and starving. Each held a spoon that reached the pot, but the spoons had handles so much longer than their own arms that they could not be used to get the stew into their mouths. The suffering was terrible.

"Come, now I will show you heaven," the Lord said after a while. They entered another room, identical to the first—the pot of stew, the group of people, the same long-handled spoons. Everyone was happy and well nourished. "I don't understand," said the man.

"Why are they happy here when they were miserable in the other room and everything was the same?"

The Lord smiled. "Ah, it is simple," he said. "Here, they have learned to feed each other."

CHAPTER 13

Meeting Elena

The day I met my wife, Elena, was one of the best days of my life. She was a fellow teacher, and we met at a staff meeting. We have been married now for over six years. She is smarter than any woman I have ever met. Intrigued by her confidence, I knew she was different because, unlike the other women I had dated; she didn't hang on every word and was not easy to impress. Let's just say, I worked hard. I proposed to her on Christmas Day surrounded by her family. They play the white elephant gift exchange every year, and her cousin and I hatched a plan for Elena to receive my gift, which was her engagement ring. It meant a lot to her to do this with her family in the same room. Our wedding was a weeklong festival complete with a mariachi band.

Her family is a close-knit group of people who have built a business out of a consistent pattern of working hard and sticking together.

Her family's business grew from the humblest of beginnings to become what is considered one of the most respected hispanic-owned-and-operated businesses in the Dallas area today.

Much of this family-based business's success can be attributed to the drive, spirit, and ingenuity of one woman: its founder, Maria

Luna. It was her vision and strong work ethic that carried her and her family through hardship to achieve a better life, while still keeping a firm hold on their values and beliefs.

At the young age of twenty-three, this recently widowed mother of two set out to make a better life for herself and her family. In the beginning, she took a job at a local grocery store on North Griffin Street just to make ends meet. As fate would have it, while she was working there, Maria came upon an opportunity to purchase a used corn grinder that had been returned to the store. Little did she know at the time that her decision would change the course of her family's lives for generations to come.

Initially, she began grinding corn for the Mexican people who lived in her area. In February of 1924, she started what would become Luna's Tortilla Factory. The location is now a Dallas landmark, but back then, it contained the hopes and dreams of a young family. With absolutely no knowledge of how to make tortillas, Maria wisely hired and learned the process from other Hispanic women in her community. At year's end, she had employed as many as twenty-five women to make over five hundred tortillas a day. Over the next several years, as business continued to grow, the little tortilla factory would have to expand. In 1939, Ms. Luna gave control of the operation to her son, who was nineteen years old and just married.

The family was so tightly knit that for many years, Mr. Luna and his wife, Alejandra, lived in an apartment over the tortilla factory, as did his mother. When he bought a home on Denton Drive in 1949, it took him two years to tell his mother that he and his wife were going to move.

All of Mr. Luna's children worked at the tortilla factory, and two are still with the company four generations later. Business is still growing.

Elena and I have a daughter, Laney, who has enriched our lives more than I ever thought possible. She has been born into a family that will teach her about hard work and doing what is right. Laney is the true "General" of my cadet corps.

CHAPTER 14

Parent Classes

As I stated before, my wife is the smartest person I know. One of my favorite ideas she came up with was to teach a parenting class on Wednesday evenings. Many of these parents spoke broken English. She taught them how to read and write basic English words. She continued teaching the parents for a whole year, and when the rubber met the road, those parents were learning alongside the children at home. I have to confess; I've never eaten so well. The parents would bring food for Elena to take home, and that was fine by me. I knew, come Wednesday evening, some good grub was coming my way. Elena was able to improve the quality of education in their households and in the classroom. At the classes, she would tell the parents how their children were doing and then they were able to help her with the discipline of those kids. If we did that across the board with parents and whatever language barriers or disadvantages they have, grades would improve and parent involvement would increase. If you take the parents of a third-generation Ivy League college student, sit down with them to talk about the curriculum, and tell them to get their child into the college prep courses, those parents will have the knowledge of how to get their children through the rigors of testing and applications because when the parents are prepared, the children are prepared.

When a parent doesn't speak English, it creates a disability for them and the child. They cannot participate in a child's education as much as they need to and notes brought home by students go unread most of the time. Students are left to do their homework with little help from their parents. They can't make informed decisions about which school placement is best for their child.

The Census Bureau data from 2008 states that among children six to seventeen who live with parents, almost one-quarter have at least one foreign-born parent. With this kind of data, it is imperative that something be done to help bridge the gap between parents and the educational process.

The Minneapolis school system started implementing a program called the Continuing Parent Education Opportunity (CPEO) at one of the Minneapolis public schools.

CPEO is a program the Minneapolis school district started in 2008 and operates in roughly twenty-eight schools (elementary through high school) each year.

According to Damon Gunn, program coordinator for the Minneapolis Public Schools Office of Family Engagement, the program has four goals:

- Gives parents a better understanding of the school system;
- Offers creative ways for parents to support their kids at home (homework help);
- Helps build relationships with parents, the school, and staff; and
- Prepares students for college.

These program goals are addressed differently depending on whether parents have children at elementary, middle, or high school levels. The elementary level looks at understanding the school system and working on building blocks, such as self-esteem. At the middle school level, the curriculum focuses on the adolescent, how to motivate a student to read and do homework, along with how to handle distractions, such as peer pressure. The high school level presents college options, testing, and financial aid.

Two facilitators lead each session. The program is available in four languages: Spanish, English, Somali, and Hmong. Handouts are also given in the language of the participants. The handouts are some of the most comprehensive materials for helping parents guide their youth to college available.

Gunn said that what participants in the program like most is the interactive setting. The learning comes from each other and not from lectures by the facilitators.

Tex Ostvig has been a CPEO facilitator for two and a half years, leading programs at each level from elementary to high school. He said the program is valuable because parents are introduced to numerous topics, such as parental engagement, academic success, positive youth development, and college access. The curriculum is a version of experiential learning that involves and engages parents from all areas of life as well as various cultural backgrounds.

"Schools are striving to make every student college ready," Ostvig said. "A successful student has the support of their school, community, and family. The partnerships of the schools and CPEO send a message to the community, youth, the parents, the families and our society, that they believe in providing a pathway to college. The program provides education to the parents in the schools that their youth are learning in. When the parents are learning, then families are learning and when that happens, the spirit of learning begins to flow from the families into the schools and the classrooms. Everyone wins, students, parents, and schools."

Upon completion of the course, parents receive a certificate of graduation from the program, a certificate for a free community education class, and the possibility for a college scholarship to the University of Minnesota. Since its debut in 2008, more than 2,700 parents have graduated from the CPEO program. Because of CPEO's success, St. Paul, Brooklyn Center, Duluth, and about seven other districts have now adopted the model or are starting this year. (Saurwein, 2011)

As you can see, whether it is a well-thought-out program like Minneapolis has in place or a small informal group of parents on a Wednesday night, the method of education for parents works and can be implemented anywhere, anytime.

CHAPTER 15

We Are All Connected

We gravitate to people just like ourselves and can instantly find things that we have in common. But when people are from different countries or don't speak the same language, we think there is no connection. The reality is we are all connected.

Having two ears and one mouth means that you are supposed to listen twice as much as you talk. For example, learning about others' family stories, things their kids do, and their background in military service or education brings us together in many aspects of our lives. When you listen to people, you are able to have a connection on a more personal level than is possible by basing your assumptions just on their appearance alone. These common bonds inspire you to feel obligated to help or get help from each other. Once, I was far from home and in an elevator with five people in Philadelphia. We went from the first floor to the sixty-third floor and not one word was spoken—until the elevator broke down and we were forced to speak to each other. After thirty minutes of talking, we all realized we had something in common. One of the men trapped with me had been stationed at the same base in Germany as I had but thirty years earlier. One woman was born in the small town where I now reside. Instantly, our six-by-six enclosure got a little more comfortable. Therefore, what would it hurt to say hello and listen to people? Nine out of ten people will say that they just want to be heard. Forming positive connections with each other can only better our society.

Narrow it down and begin to influence your little piece of earth, and you will realize how much you can change this world. As adults, it's hard for us to step out of our comfort zone and meet new people, to form new relationships and really find out if we are like-minded. I think it's easier with kids, which brings me to the idea of pairing up those like-minded students.

CHAPTER 16

Come Together

If you bring together like-minded students and encourage them by assigning them the same schedule throughout the day, they will be more focused and achieve greater educational success. For example, I may have thirty cadets in my first-period class who are outstanding for me; when I release them to their other classes however, they are usually with kids who are not in the program. If the school is in a neighborhood with a lot of crime, they may revert to being disrespectful just to impress their neighborhood friends who may not have the same goals in mind, instead of staying with the values they were taught in the previous class. What if we took those thirty cadets and, from first period, kept them all together; they all go to a science class, then English, then history, lunch, physical education, and so on. Now, we can take the thirty kids and track their attendance, performance, and test scores and at the end of the year, show that those thirty kids outperformed everyone in the building. What about band, drama, sports, dance, and engineering groups, to name a few? This is already being done by way of space camps, baseball camps, and even writing groups, and it works. Guess what; the kids from the neighborhood would have to find something to belong to so they could be part of a group.

How about the student who doesn't play sports and isn't interested in Leadership Cadet Corps or anything, but he or she likes mechanics? Well, uniting kids throughout the day with similar interests can benefit the school and the students. I'm not just talking about tracking their performance for that one year that they're together; I'm talking about implementing a tracking system that will be able to ensure their enrollment in college.

Tracking students would have been of great value to me in high school. We need to focus more on following the students from day one of high school until graduation and beyond.

Counselors are busy with mapping out schedule changes all year long. Having the teachers tracking the students' performance or academic trajectory ensures the chance of graduation as well as enrollment in college. The future of our country is dependent upon the young people graduating from college and entering into the world with the knowledge and skills college provides. For example, say we track Claire in the tenth grade by recommending an academic career plan. By her junior year, we know her ranking and are working with her so she fits into a percentile that qualifies her for grants and scholarships. "Our" investment in her future should be motivation for her to keep up her end of the bargain. There is no sense of entitlement. When senior year is almost over, we help her navigate the paperwork related to college applications and enrollment. Just because we can graduate 60 percent of students from high school and 30 percent go to college, that doesn't mean they will graduate from college. Out of that 30 percent, how many drop out after the first year? Maybe no one was motivating them. They then go to a community college and have to take remedial classes, but do not see any light at the end of the tunnel. They join the workforce and start making more money than ever before, even though it is a relatively small amount. They stop going to school and work at tire store, for example, and then start a family. They find themselves more educated yet in the same predicament that their parents and grandparents were in when they first began. Every student can go to college, but it doesn't seem as if every student is graduating from college. Tracking provides guidance and direction for a student in hopes of ensuring everyone a better life.

The American dream is for people to come to this country, work, and have a better life than their parents did. We can take those children and provide the education they will require as they enter into the real world. The first child goes to community college and then to the four-year university; his sister goes straight to the four-year university; and the little brother ends up going to an Ivy League college. That is in one generation.

Colleen Lowry, a teacher in Dallas, believes an easy way to track students without added cost, is for teachers in high school to keep the same students multiple years. She believes if we can keep the same students ninth through eleventh grades, we will be more effective in making sure we build stronger relationships and keep kids from dropping out, which will keep them on track for their future. Having spoken to master teachers over the course of thirteen years, I believe these ideas may work in every school system.

CHAPTER 17

Making and Saving Money for Schools

Schools can find innovative ways to save money and increase revenue for those crucial programs and items necessary to keep districts running efficiently.

A Store

More school districts should have their own school store. The proceeds would go back to the school and help with an array of needs, such as new cafeteria tables, play-yard equipment, or locker-room renovations. Nonprofit school stores make sense, and the parents are very willing to shop there, even if it's not the most convenient, because it benefits their child's school. Many schools in urban settings have a uniform policy that is a standardized dress code, consisting of polo shirts and khaki pants. Why outsource those uniforms, when we can sell them in the school store and make money for the children?

Some benefits of an online school store include:

- Convenience

When a student discovers he or she doesn't have the material needed for class, he or she can easily run to the store and purchase that item, from pens and pencils to extra paper, without having to borrow from fellow classmates.

- Fundraising and Service

A school store can serve two purposes: raise money for the school and provide a service that is convenient for both students and parents. Since the workers are volunteers, the overhead is low. Who wants to go to three or four different stores to find the proper dress code items when, in one day, parents can be done with their shopping?

- Customized Service

The store can be tailored for the school's particular needs. If a teacher requires specialized equipment in a subject, such as earth science, the store can sell the specific project kits designed for that task. It saves money and time. How many parents have gone to an arts supply place and wandered aimlessly looking for items that are not available or are out of stock because of the large number of students in that school district working on similar projects?

- *Student Training*

Students should be encouraged to work in the store because it helps them develop communication skills and gets them involved in the business end of profit making. The more students are exposed to people, especially fellow students, the more they become comfortable and gain self-confidence working with others.

Advertising

Why not sell every baseball diamond in your school district, large or small, to companies for advertising. The monetary residuals will continue for years. In Mt. Airy, North Carolina, they raised money by selling commemorative bricks to line the walkway leading to the field. More and more these days, we see how almost every major sporting venue is named after a company—American Airlines Center, Lincoln Financial Field, to name a couple. There is no reason why your local ball field can't be named Joe's Auto Parts Field or Boston Market Stadium. That company now feels a sense of pride and may do something for opening day or championship games. Once that happens, other local businesses pitch in. I remember our local restaurant giving 20 percent of its proceeds to the school one Wednesday a month. Most companies have money in their budgets for local advertising. Parents can get involved by asking their car repair shop, dentist, or insurance company to advertise. It's another way to bring the schools and businesses together to work toward the betterment of the community.

Transportation

Most sports fields do not have lights; therefore, almost all teams have to travel earlier in the day without buses, which are busy taking children home. Many school districts rent vans and transport the players and coaching staff to each game. This is done, on average, fifteen times a year, and that's just for one sport, in one school.

Purchasing two vans for each campus would save thousands of dollars a year, per district. The district would be in charge of maintaining regular oil changes and gas, keeping things controlled and simple. For example, a baseball season for one school, on average, in van rentals, costs $4,500.00. A van costs $20,000.00. You can see it doesn't take long to recover the money spent for the van, and it could be used for all the other sports throughout the school year except football, because most football teams on average are too large to travel with just two vans. A school bus costs eighty dollars per hour for the first two hours and forty dollars an hour for every hour after that, which is even more costly than renting a van. We purchased a van for LCC competitions, and in one year's time, it paid for itself. District officials in Plainfield, Illinois, recently approved the purchase of vans for their school district. The estimated savings are projected to be between $22,600 and $42,900 per year. If you compare the price of $105,000 a year to transport students to after-school programs by commissioning outside rental companies with the cost of a couple of vans, the savings are clear.

Maintenance

Custodians are hired for each campus within the school district to clean that campus. When a custodian puts a work order for something that is broken in a downtown school, he or she calls the central office and a maintenance worker is dispatched to that campus, looks at the problem, puts an order in for the materials, and, if all goes well, has it fixed with a turnaround time of approximately a week or two. The total charge, including driving time and gas, is double the amount it would be if the maintenance worker were on sight at the local school. Upfront costs would be minimal, a toolbox and a lawn mower, for example. Also, little changes like mowing the lawn once every ten days instead of seven or waxing the floors once a semester instead of the standard two would be a good start toward saving a few dollars. With an in-house maintenance person, the jobs would be done more efficiently and the grounds would be well kept because that staffer would take pride in his or her "territory." When something is your responsibility, you take care of it just a little bit more.

Professional Development

Another way to save money may be found in staff development. Many school districts require teachers to complete twenty-one hours every summer. The district has to pay to keep the building open and custodians present and pay instructors to teach the classes and for prep time. On top of that, they have to pay staff to sit in the hallway and greet people coming to the development meetings and then to print out certificates at the end. This happens at multiple sites within school districts. If you polled teachers, not many would say they learned anything they would implement in their classrooms. They would also tell you that being forced to take certain hours doesn't motivate a teacher to want to learn. The mind-set is to complete the hours required and be done with it. Staff development is only useful if applied.

One solution is illustrated by a recent LCC staff development session. The teachers ran a camp over the summer. The time was applied to their hours required. They did activities and confidence-building courses to benefit the kids, got credit, and completed their hours. They also had time to pick the brains of the other instructors who were there helping them run the camp. I am not saying that everyone needs to run a camp with kids, but we can find other ways to mitigate the costs of this training. We could follow the trend of offering online courses and printing certificates from our home printers. It could save tens of thousands of dollars. Having teachers choose what they want to learn will be more beneficial in the classroom because they will choose instructional methods that can be applied where needed, inside their own classrooms.

Textbooks

Large amounts of money are spent on textbooks. A textbook costs approximately sixty dollars. School systems do not just buy a few books. Instead of asking the teachers what they need, the school district looks to the enrollment for that year. For instance, literature teachers do not necessarily use their books. They assign book reports and essays. Why not take orders from the teachers who know best how many they will need? Many teachers rely on a multitude of resources to complete their studies. With access to the Internet, teachers are pulling worksheets and study guides from many different sites and printing as needed. Alternatively, more schools are going high tech and replacing traditional textbooks with e-readers. This idea has some flaws in that the cost of these e-readers and the downloads may be more than the physical textbooks themselves. However, efficiency and the ability to swap out books will only improve as technology goes forward, and let's not forget the environmental dilemma of using trees for paper. A conservation website called conserveatree.org estimates that a forty-foot tree yields only about 8,300 pages of treated paper. That equates to less than twelve textbooks for an entire tree. If a college student went all four years toward a degree, he or she would use approximately six trees' worth of textbooks. Almost nineteen million students intend on going to college within the next year.

Currently, boxes of books, brand new and unused, sit in our schools. Textbooks are important, but someone can figure out how to save money in this new age where everyone has a touch-screen gadget. Donating old textbooks to developing countries through local charities is a great way to save money. It's a program that has worked for many years by saving on hauling fees, but it is often underutilized.

Another way to save money is to consolidate computer programs used for logging grades. Many school districts have two or three systems—one for attendance, one for grades, and another for emails. Consolidation to one system would save money and time.

Trust

Another unique and effective way to make money for your school is called "Trust Your Interest." The district would find a donor who would allow the district to borrow his or her money, as opposed to donating it, for one year. The catch is the loan is interest free. The district would invest those funds and keep the interest proceeds. After one year, the donor would get all his or her money back. The reason this works over a donation or handout is simple: if you ask a millionaire if he or she will donate a million dollars to the school district for programs, he or she will probably say no. But what if you asked to borrow those funds for a year? At the end of that year, you would give the money back in full, insured only by a signed contract with collateral attachments. Then the district would invest and keep only the interest from that money. More potential donors would be likely to say yes to this request. Sizable donations are rare compared to loans for a specific period. The paperwork is minimal. Often, the act of donating money for a year tends to snowball and more people follow. This also places a "put your money where your mouth is" effect on the millionaire and billionaire company owners in large cities who say they want their school districts to succeed and for their cities to be the best in the country. In essence, they will get more bang for their buck by helping our schools as opposed to paying a few thousand every five to ten years for a new swing set at the elementary school. They will be able to see the school district thrive for years by allowing it to make money from their money.

CHAPTER 18

The Museum

The ten thousand dollars Mr. and Mrs. Coker gave me did more than just get me started. It got me thinking. We won national championships, and that was great for the program as well as the school. We completed community projects, and that was wonderful for our surrounding area. But now we had a chance to do something for the country. Building a military history museum would benefit hundreds of thousands of Americans, and here is how. The museum on our campus would play host to free school field trips; elementary school kids could come and learn about the wars our country has been engaged in throughout the years. High school kids would be inspired to write essays, to join the service, and finally to realize what their grandparents and great-grandparents went through.

My middle school students would gain a wealth of knowledge by acting as historians, curators, and tour guides. As for the men and women who served, they could finally take their treasures out of the attic and place them on display. So we started to build. We made a viral video asking for donated military gear, display cases, and, of course, funds for the construction of the building. As the months went by, slowly but surely, the money came in. Faster than anything else, we received donations for the museum collection.

There was a different veteran at our door every day with something from his or her past to place in the museum. We received uniforms, medals, plaques, and helmets from all over the country. As the students researched and cataloged the items donated, they found one common denominator among them all: each of the individuals had not only served his or her country with honor but had stayed inside a Quonset hut at one point or another during their tenure in the service. There was no doubt in our minds what the museum structure was going to look like. On May 8, 2012, we opened a military history museum on a middle school campus. The date was easy for me to select because it was my daughter's fifth birthday. What better way to incorporate my life's work than with the birthday of my ultimate motivator, Laney Bates.

The day went off without a hitch. Over five hundred guests, one thousand students, and countless veterans, from as far back as World War II, were in attendance. It even came complete with a helicopter fly-over. When asked, "Why did you do it?" my response has been and will always be, "Why not?"